A COSMIC SURGERY

A story of *ABUSE*, *TRAUMA*, and finding *PEACE* through Psychedelic *MEDICINE*

Written by Jose Torres & Rev. Dr. Maureen Hoyt

This book is dedicated to my Samantha.
You are the strongest person I know. Your love, patience,
and faith was the lighthouse guiding me home.

I am forever grateful to Dr. Rev. Maureen Hoyt ♥.
You were able to decipher my madness and make it flow.

The story you are about to read is true. Read it with an open heart so that you may find your own Truth, through whatever madness you are facing.

So, *hang on to your calzones*, I'm about to take you on a magical journey, through hell and back.

INTRODUCTION
A COSMIC SURGERY

When Jose asked me to co-write this book with him, I was surprised and flattered. I asked him why he chose me. He said, "After working with you in counseling, you know me better than anyone else, except maybe Samantha." And yes, there were some experiences he shared with me at the outset of our time together he never shared with her until after he visited The POI Institute in Cabo San Lucas.

I am a Religious Science minister since 1993 with a Doctor of Divinity and a Doctor of Religious Science. I was a pulpit minister from 1993 to 2016 when I "retired" and went back to my roots in editing and proof-reading. About the same time, my counseling/coaching business began to thrive as well, and because of the Law of Attraction, people struggling with addiction seemed to find their way to me. Perhaps, it was because I saw their spiritual essence as perfect, whole, and complete, or I could relate to their addictive personality or . . . you name it.

Jose was in the midst of the worst part of his addiction when he first came to me. At that point, I'd known him for about eight years, and when I found out in our first meeting that he was an alcoholic, I remember thinking, *wow, he hides it well.* In fact, he may have mustered the courage to show up for his first appointment by being inebriated! His choosing to come to me was the beginning of his healing. Even though Samantha gave him an ultimatum to come to me, he had to decide to dress up and show up to fulfil his agreement. His wanting a relationship with her was greater than his fear of divulging who he feared he was. This was the beginning of his journey into his "dark" side. We all have one but most of us never act on it. Stephen King, the author, has made a fortune exploring his dark side as have many other writers who don't show it in real life.

About two years ago, a good friend shared a Tim Ferriss interview with Gabor Mate, a Canadian medical doctor, whose family emigrated to Canada around 1956 during the Hungarian Revolution. When he was younger, Dr. Mate's mother said to him, "Be a doctor; you'll always have a job." Dr. Mate's work with addiction brought him to the conclusion that alcohol or drug addiction is *not* a disease as we've been led to believe in the 12-Step Program; it is a coping mechanism for trauma we've experienced. That idea of trauma has many definitions – PTSD, physical abuse, sexual abuse, emotional abuse, etc. Jose had all of them. Dr. Mate uses hallucinogens, such as Ayahuasca, to get to the root of the deeply subjectified experience causing one to resort to alcohol or drugs. The interview with Tim Ferriss is a long one – 2 hours and 30 minutes or so, but I watched it all the way through and was mesmerized by its candor.

As a child of the 60s, I experimented with lots of recreational drugs. Diet pills were my drug of choice along with marijuana and alcohol. I got clean from amphetamines in the early 70s and didn't smoke marijuana after that; however, I continued drinking up until January 1994 when I finally achieved sobriety. Many of my clients today are or have been alcohol and drug addicted, and in learning this about them, I send them the link to Dr. Mate's interview with Tim Ferriss. I did this with Jose, and after listening to almost every YouTube video and TED Talk, Jose began his own exploration of where and how he could engage in similar treatment, He discovered the POI Institute.

In this book, he chronicles his journey of self-discovery. Before he went to Mexico, we did some really in-depth work together in our counseling sessions which, I believe, set the tone for him to take the leap of faith and get on that airplane to Cabo. His divulging certain information to me was a lot less confrontive than he thought it would be. So, I feel he was primed and ready to let go of whatever trauma he suffered to become a clean and sober individual, living a superlative life with the love of his life, changing his physical demeanor, while becoming a valuable and generous contributor to the lives of others through his volunteer work and his commitment to give back.

He says I "fired" him as a client, and he's right about that. People come into our lives for a reason, a season, or a lifetime. Jose is a lifer in my circle of influence. The healing and subsequent transformation of Jose Torres speaks clearly about his willingness to be who he is truly meant to be and who he is still becoming. He, like all of us, is God's masterpiece, but he is still a work in progress because the rest of his story is yet to unfold.

Rev. Dr. Maureen Hoyt, Minister, Counsellor, and Coach

PROLOGUE
A COSMIC STORY

The "Makers Mark and Double IPA" guys were back! Jose and his colleagues that came to dine at Oggi's in Garden Grove were in town. I happened to be their waiter on the first night and was requested exclusively the next two nights because I never cut them off. I was able to handle their trash talk and give it right back. They appreciated it. Man these guys could drink. It was impressive. We always had a good time. Jose would end the evening with, *see you next year.*

Sure enough, a year later the same crew walked in and I knew it was on. I gave the bartender a heads up, these guys were **crazy**. I had recently started training in Brazilian Jiu-Jitsu and developed some serious cauliflower ears. Coincidentally, Jose started around the same time and showed up with swollen cauliflower ears as well. What were the odds? Several Makers Mark shots later followed by three 8.2% Double IPA, we exchanged information and I invited Jose to come train at my school Hustle Brazilian Jitsu in Santa Ana, CA with Professor Russel Cantorna, a GI and NO-GI World Champion.

Jose took me up on it and showed up one day. He was surprised at the level of intensity of our training. We are a competition school and Jose trained with a bunch of hobbyists in Simi Valley. Poor guy almost had a heart attack. I recommended that he switch over to Checkmat Northridge under Professor Arnaldo Maidana, who was an active competitor and also a GI and NO-GI World Champion. I had planted the seed and it worked. In the summer of 2020, he joined Checkmat. His transformation was now in progress.

On Nov 7th 2020 Jose, four teammates, and I competed at a local Jiu-Jitsu tournament in Phoenix, AZ. He ended up not making weight but the guy working the event noticed he was old and just let it slide. He was a deer in headlights once he stepped on the mats and lost badly. That night we went out to a local bar and got hammered. A few of us threw up, including Jose. It was a shit show. That was the last time I shared a drink with him.

Even though he had lost, this event motivated him to commit to taking his Jiu-Jitsu to the next level. He turned into a training machine after that weekend. He started training Jiu-Jitsu every morning, lifting weights in the evenings, and booking private sessions. I even asked him if he was training for the Olympics! He was determined.

It was amazing to see his progress. I couldn't believe his transformation. Jose is now full of life, one year sober, down 50lbs, and an American National Jiu-Jitsu Champion beating guys 25lbs heavier than him. He is now a better father, a better husband, a better friend, and now a role model to others. He is even learning to play the drums, skateboarding, and now writing a damn book.

Way to lead by example and change your life for the better my bro. We can all learn a thing or two from your journey. It is truly inspiring!

Dory "The Lebanese Tiger" Aoun
@DoryAoun
Checkmat Purple Belt under Professor Russel Cantorna
2021 NO-GI World Champion
2020 American National GI and NO-GI World Champion
2 x Pan American Champion
4 x American National Champion
Previous #1 Ranked IBJJF Blue Belt

For those who are in the struggle, the night
is darkest just before the dawn.
And I promise you, the dawn is coming.

ALPHA

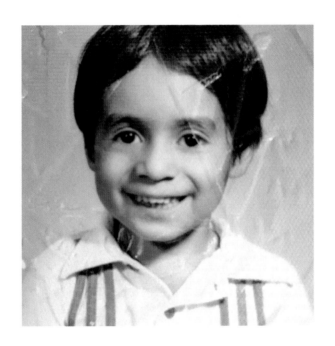

PART ONE
ALPHA

So, I guess this is the beginning of my story.

Let's get started.

I was born in Sonsonate, El Salvador in March 1977, to my mother Carmen and my father Francisco. He was 22 years old when he had me, the same age I was when my daughter, Celeste, was born. My sister Patty was two years older.

My dad left to go to the United States shortly after I was born. The last time I saw my biological mother was when I was two years old. One day, she left and never returned. El Salvador was in a state of chaos due to its Civil War, and we had been abandoned by our parents.

My grandfather, "Chico Lion," raised us. He was a kind and loving man and took care of me and my sister as best he could, even though he struggled with alcoholism. In 1980, my grandfather, sister, and I relocated to the States. We were refuges of war...

While living a new life in Los Angeles, CA, my father had remarried. Rosa was her name, and they had a beautiful daughter, Reina.

My dad *forgot* to tell his new wife about my sister and me. So when my grandfather dropped us off at his door step, we were a huge surprise to her. Like it or not, Rosa's family suddenly grew from one child to three. From that day forward, we felt a huge resentment on the part of my new stepmother. She hated us. Patty and I took a backseat to everything for our entire childhood.

My dad struggled to make ends meet. He was always broke. Always angry and drinking a lot. He beat Patty and me daily and called me names. **Faggot**, **stupid idiot**, and **pussy** were his favorites. The abuse continued my entire childhood throughout high school. He was a drunk asshole!

A few years later, they had two more children. Kimmy and Marco. I became their protector. I stood at the door of all my father's frustrations. His rage. No child deserved to live how I was living, and even at a young age, I took it upon myself to take all the beatings to protect them.

My dad got by on his personality and good looks. He was skilled as a welder and would often build toys for us that were pretty cool.

His alcohol addiction affected him so much that he could never hold down a job for long. Financially, we were unstable. He would spend his money partying and hanging out with assholes on the weekends. We moved a lot in those days because we would get kicked out of our apartment. *He* didn't pay rent on time. Koreatown (Los Angeles) was our home.

Life sucked back in those days.

His physical abuse was getting worse. No one at school questioned where the bruises on my body came from. No one cared.

Reina, Kimmy, and Marco were the favorites. All three went to private school. Patty and I went to public school. All three went to college. There was no money for our tuition. Patty and I got the leftovers.

The constant beatings were rough, but for me, the hardest thing was the lack of love. We were never **hugged**. We were never told, "**I Love You.**" Zero **encouragement**. Only "*You're a faggot, fucking idiot, and a pussy.*"

At times, I wished I had been left in El Salvador to die in the jungle as an orphan.

As I got older, he weaponized his abuse. He'd use his belt, a bat, and his fists on me. One time, he broke Patty's nose at the dinner table. She must have chewed too loudly. He grabbed her by the back of her head and slammed her face into the table breaking her nose. There was blood everywhere.

Usually, the abuse happened behind closed doors; however, there was one incident I remember to this day, clear as day. A good family friend came to visit. Shortly after, my dad arrives home from his weekly binge and decides to beat the shit out of me in front of her. He was kicking me in the stomach, in my chest, and in my face. She tried to get him to stop but he kept at it until his "buzz" wore off. She was so traumatized that she never came back.

Every friend my dad had was an alcoholic, a scumbag, and an asshole. I was in a lot of physical and emotional pain in those days. You'd think the environment we were in couldn't get worse but it did. Say hello to my step grandmother and her piece of shit son, Denis, the drug dealer.

Everything was completely different after they showed up. My step grandmother was an evil, fucking bitch. She would shove, pinch, and slap me. I didn't feel safe in my own home. Her son was a predator, especially toward my sister. Fuck!

I would make sure not to leave her side when Denis was around. He would grab her and touch her everywhere. I would hit him, bite him, anything to stop him from touching her. I needed to protect her but I couldn't. I was only 10 years old. I tried to tell my dad but he wouldn't listen; he was too drunk. My step mother said, "You're a fucking liar!" Nobody believed us.

He ended up getting arrested and got himself deported back to El Salvador. He died in El Salvador years later of AIDS. To this day, my sister suffers with PTSD from that experience. I hope he suffered.

My dad's behavior was becoming dark. One time, I ran away from home because I could no longer bear the abuse. When my dad eventually found me, he beat the shit out of me. This time, I called him a coward. It was the worst thing I could think to call him. "You fucking coward! How can you hit me, put me down all the time, and call yourself a dad! You're supposed to protect me, not destroy me." He just stood there listening to what I was saying. And then without hesitation, he beat me even harder.

I was afraid of my father. He would remind me that he could easily kill me, go to jail, and it would be worth it. I was pretty sure he meant it, too. My stepmother knew that, and so, she would manipulate me through fear. She'd threaten me, "You'd better do this, or I'm gonna tell your dad when he gets home." Waiting for the inevitable beatings caused me tremendous anxiety. My stepmother took perverse pleasure in watching me suffer.

My coping skill for my miserable life was to become a class clown. I would use humor to avoid the humiliation when someone would notice my bruises or ripped clothes. I created an alter ego to survive. I would show up to school wearing the same pants and the same shirt for days; it was embarrassing.

I was made fun of a lot back then.

My younger siblings wore uniforms; they looked sharp. I wore Pro-Wings shoes from Payless and shopped at El Piojito (A Ghetto WalMart)

In Junior High School, I joined the school band and played the trumpet. I loved music. I was good at it.

As I mentioned earlier, I was a class clown. One day I was getting set to perform a solo in the auditorium. I was in the back waiting for my turn to go up on the stage. I noticed a kid eating a chocolate bar, and being the jackass that I was, I snatched the entire chocolate bar out of his hands and ate the whole thing. I was laughing my ass off. He stared at me kinda weird and walked away. I remember it being very thin and tasting like chocolate mint. Finally, it's my turn to go on stage. My first trumpet solo. Center stage. Let's GO!

All of a sudden, I get the bubble guts. MOTHER FUCKER! I dropped my trumpet and ran to the bathroom, making it just in time. I sat on the toilet for hours, miserable. It turns out that the kid with the chocolate was having constipation issues, and what he was eating was **EXLAX**. He was breaking off a little square to eat, and I ate the whole fuckin' bar. I never stole chocolate again!

In eighth grade, the school organized a track meet. I said to myself *I bet I could do that,* so I signed up, and I ran my first race. It was 800 meters. The gun goes off, and I found myself in second place. The guy ahead trips and falls right in front of me. Holy shit! I tried to jump over him, landed on his back, accidentally kicked him in the ribs, and won the race!

That day, I fell in love with running ☺

EGO

PART TWO
EGO

Birmingham High School Braves

First day of High School and I have pimples. Big fuckin' pimples! Fuck me! I was so skinny . . . like 100 lbs. skinny.

I ditched the trumpet and became a distance runner. As a Freshman, I made the Varsity teams in both Cross Country and Track & Field. My nickname was "Sancudo" (Mosquito). At first, I hated the name. But, in the end, it was a pretty bad ass name.

Man, I loved running! I was good at it. The afterschool and weekend tournaments kept me away from home. Away from my father. The comradery in the team gave me a sense of belonging.

As a competitive runner, I accomplished the following:

16:01 5K High School Course Record (1991)

800M 1:55

Mile 4:26

2 Mile 9:50

5K 15:24

Marathon 3:15

City Champs

XC State Championships x 3 times

Nationally ranked.

Lots of Trophies

Lots of Medals

Lots of Awards

My dad never attended my races. Ever. He showed up only at the awards ceremonies at the end of each season. To show off his star athlete and take credit for my success. What an asshole!

I was Olympic quality. Enough to get multiple scholarships to college, but I was a coward. The low self-esteem kept me from achieving my potential. Things were bad at home, and I needed to escape.

I decided to quit running and join the military instead.

I'm sorry, Coach King. I know you tried.

United States Marines

This was a kick ass experience.

I got to blow shit up, travel, be a jarhead, drill, hump, cook, shoot, and DRINK LOTS OF ALCOHOL.

Lessons learned that stuck with me till this day: Strong Work Ethic, Patriotism, Camaraderie, Efficiency, and Dark Humor!

From the Halls of Montezuma
To the shores of Tripoli
We fight our country's battles
In the air, on land, and sea.

If the Army and the Navy
Ever look on Heaven's scenes,

They will find the streets are guarded
By United States Marines.

OORAH!

SEMPER FIDELIS

El Cholo

Being a waiter at El Cholo was so cool. I made a lot of money getting people fucked up on Cadillac Margaritas. A lot of hot women. A lot of free booze. A lot of excess. I loved working there.

I was recently married to a hot young bride and had a new born daughter, Celeste. I have to admit, marriage was challenging. I had no fuckin' clue what I was doing. I had to be a husband, a father, a man at twenty two years old. I needed to earn enough money to put a roof over our heads, feed us, buy a car, pay bills, and be an adult.

No one had ever showed me what to do. So instead of asking for advice, I just repeated behavior patterns I observed from my dad. My drinking escalated. I would hang out with assholes, scum bags, and alcoholics. I would spend most of my earnings on *entertaining my peeps*. Margaritas, Chips and Salsa, and Tequila shots.

Shortly after, I was introduced to my new best friend, **Cocaine**. It fueled my shenanigans. My wife found out and gave me an ultimatum. Either I clean up my act or I would have to leave.

I fucked up and got fired, spent five days in Jail for a DUI, then later, we divorced.

Fuck me...

B-BIZ

I started working a legit job as a customer service rep, making $12.50 an hour. I loved the owner. We had a lot in common. He nurtured my business acumen. I went from a customer service rep to Director of Sales in 10 years. I was the shit. Now making six figures. I got to travel the world. Selling things. That was fun.

Being a weekend dad sucked. It was Sizzler, Blockbuster, Mac and Cheese, and Broccoli. But I cherished every other weekend I got to spend time with my baby girl.

Along came the hottest chick I had ever seen, Samantha Cosney. She had a great ass. I fell in love... I climbed the side of a building once to impress her. Nearly killed myself. I couldn't keep my hands off her.

The owner of the company I worked for died. My drinking escalated once again. I missed the funeral over a fuckin' meeting. That hurt me more than I thought it would.

Samantha and I moved in together. Better yet, I moved in with her.

I asked her to marry me. She said yes.

I got fired, again.

Out of spite, I started a business and became a direct competitor to my former employer. Unfortunately, Samantha was still working for my rival and was given an ultimatum: break up with me or get fired. *Conflict of interest, I guess.* Fuck them!

I told her it was either me or them.

She made her choice. She was fired.

She worked so long to achieve a good career only to throw it away for my insecurities. She should have fired me instead. *I was such a coward.*

Then Alejandro enters the picture. He was a long-time friend who was a successful business owner in Venezuela. An extremely intelligent man.

One day, I want to be like him! I remember saying to myself.

Alejandro was eager to help me grow my business. In fact, he wanted to be a partner and invited me to travel to China to attend trade shows and meet people who would help me succeed. To be honest, I was drunk most of the time. All I remember were hangovers.

Alejandro was *showing me the ropes.* I was becoming an entrepreneur. A business owner. A CEO. He asked me again to be a business partner, I said, "Let me think about it."

I get a call from my accountant, Greg. "We need to talk."

I get a call from Samantha. "We need to talk."

I get a call from Alejandro. "We need to talk."

I let them go to voicemail.

I was too drunk to care.

Once I sobered up, I told Alejandro NO THANKS and brought on another business partner. I had a good friend who was always driving expensive cars, carried cash in his pockets, and owned several houses. I wanted to become successful like him. So I gave away half of my business to him. I trusted him. After all, he was my *good friend.*

Boy, was I wrong! He was a con artist. I made all the money, and he spent it on stupid shit! BMWs, 30th floor office space in downtown LA, dinners, champagne, and more debt. What an asshole!

CIRCA: JAN 2010
Consumer Electronics Show (CES)
Las Vegas, Nevada

What a shit show!

By this time, I accumulated lots of debt. Well, Samantha accumulated a lot of debt, too. She piled on $60,000 in credit card debt because I had no credit. If only I had saved and reinvested in the company, rather than allow unnecessary expenses, we would have been fine.

I spent it ALL!

I remember telling Samantha, "Trust me, the check is in the mail." No check. Just more bar tab receipts.

Our relationship suffered. I hated her for making me feel guilty.

I refused to talk to her. Love her. Be intimate with her.

I was full of rage, and I tried to make it Samantha's fault.

SPIRITS

PART THREE
SPIRITS

Told by my Addiction ...

Hello.

I am the destroyer of Worlds. You can call me **Addiction**.

I had been dying to meet Jose for YEARS, and we finally got to meet in person on January 7, 2010.

There was something special about him; I was actually nervous.

Seduction was my game, and the agreement I proposed was simple. I promised him the world, a new world where he could escape from the chaos in his life. Escape from his girlfriend. Escape from his company. Escape from his responsibilities. Escape from the fear. Escape from the pain. Escape from himself.

A contract was signed. *Not really. I scribbled fuck you on a napkin, and he smiled and signed it. He was too drunk to notice. I wiped my ass with it 10 minutes later.*

He invited me to his home. I met his family, close friends, and loved ones. I put on a *nice smile*. Even hugged them all.

My goal was simple. To fuck with everything he held dear - his girlfriend, his friendships, his finances, his appearance, his health, his mind, his body, his soul. I would destroy them all!

As I mentioned earlier, there was something special about him. I'd already spent time with his father, his grandfather, and generations before them. But HE was the one whom I've been waiting for. He was gifted with a brilliant mind, a weak ego, and the experience of lots of rage. The perfect mark.

I went to work quickly.

Let's talk about the things I accomplished with Jose.

- His girlfriend hated him.
- His friends no longer trusted him.
- His health was deteriorating.
- I made him hang out with sick minded individuals.
- I showed him how to be a Master Manipulator (*my best works yet*)
- He gave up coaching
- I poisoned his mind
- He became a psychopath

But let's focus in my top three

1. The Girlfriend
2. Manipulation
3. Psychosis

The Girlfriend:

Samantha was a stubborn gal. She would not let me have any fun. Always delaying my progress. Therefore, I made her life a living hell.

She could no longer trust him. I made her feel miserable. I riddled her body with pain. All the friends he had were assholes. She hated him for bringing them into her home.

I was not done with her, yet!

Jose was a complete fuckin' mess. He tried getting rid of me many times, but my claws were dug deep in him. I was not going anywhere.

He would always put on his childhood trauma mask and begged Samantha to stay. He said he would change for her.

But Samantha was always one step ahead of me. Always encouraging him to find help. She was a worthy adversary.

Give HIM to me.

He is MINE.

ALL MINE!

However, I am a patient monster. I have all the time in the world.

Samantha has a strong spirit, though, and it makes me... *never mind.*

Manipulation:

His ego was a perfect disguise. His brilliant mind made everything function.

In AA meetings, people would talk about being a functional alcoholic. Baby, he was off the charts! MENSA qualified.

He was on autopilot, and I was running the show.

Denial, denial, denial was my motto. Whatever he got blamed for, I denied it. He always turned to me for comfort.

I will make you feel better, my child. **What a faggot!**

It's okay. You are a stud. You are successful. You drive a BMW. You're the CEO. You have an amazing body. All the women want you. You know Jiu-Jitsu. **What a stupid idiot!**

I will never abandon you like your mother. I will never hurt you like your father. **What a pussy!**

Here, have a drink...

He was a smooth talker. A natural salesman with a great smile. A black belt in the art of manipulation.

I showed him how to hide his drinking in plain sight.

I helped him create multiple personalities. One for the girlfriend. One for his friends. One for his profession. One for his drinking. One for the shadows.

His word contained no honor.

He sold his soul for Double IPAs and shots of Maker's.

Psychosis:

Jose was too smart. He was able to look at something or someone and reverse-engineer them. He would figure out how they worked. Their strengths and weaknesses. Then use that data to manipulate them. If he studied and applied himself, he could have become a Psychologist of some sort. Interestingly enough, you know who else shares those same personality traits and mindset? Serial Killers!

So, I then conceived this brilliant idea! To nurture the latter.

Bienvenue à l'Université de la destruction!

His teacher was my bestie, Death.

They hit it off instantly.

Let's look at the curriculum:

- Blending In
- Smiles 101
- Manipulation
- Multiple Personalities
- Deception
- Seduction

I then sent him to private contractors to understand the following topics:

- Psychology
- Weaponology
- Reverse Engineering
- Killing

He graduated with honors.

An offer was made, and he accepted.

I gave him a huge signing bonus and a three month vacation so he could rest. I needed him fresh.

He had important work to do.

The Job Description:

To hunt and kill pedophiles.

Ladies and Gents. I give you, my new VP of Retribution, Jose, the Psychopath. It was time to hunt!

DING! Sorry kids, our time is up.

It's been fun, but I have to run.

I have an appointment to meet my bro, Death, at the local liquor store. We seem to be running low on wine, beer, and *Spirits*. **Cheers!**

SILENCE

PART FOUR

SILENCE

Told by Samantha

In early 2008, Jose and I became engaged. I started jotting down ideas for my vows, and I remember writing that our relationship was like a walk through a lovely park. Unfortunately, it became my walk through the valley of the shadow of death!

I was fired from the job that was the pinnacle of my career at the end of 2009. A few months after, Jose became withdrawn. He began drinking more and retreated into himself. I sat in the same room with him for years, alone. We didn't interact with each other because he bought an iPad and started playing games with strangers. So, in resignation, I picked up my own device and started playing solitaire. *If ya can't beat 'em, join 'em.* There we sat. Together but separate, in our own worlds.

I must say, it wasn't all bad. We enjoyed a lot of good times over the years: entertaining, going out, and once we started to stabilize financially, going on trips. Most of the time, we got along well and *pretended* everything was fine. Metaphorically, we strolled through that lovely park again. My observations about the sober Jose: He has a heart of gold and a beautiful soul, and he would do anything for people in general, random people, and his family in particular. I have always been impressed with how sweet he is with his daughter especially after he suffered such abuse growing up. I admired him for not continuing the abuse cycle.

Throughout the years, however, there were the many times Jose's drinking increased, and he went through periods of daily binges. He was full of rage, which he often directed at me and would say the most hurtful things! It was usually at this point Jose would take action to quit drinking. I'm an eternal optimist and knew we would get through this; unfortunately, we always ended up in the same place. His drinking started again, just a little at first, then it escalated until he snowballed out of control. During one discussion about his drinking, Jose said, "I drank when we started dating. Why is it a problem for you now?" I told him something changed, something was different about the drinking and him. Years of frustrating, confusing times. During the periods of his binging, Jose would act like he hated me, I *felt* his hate, yet he would still talk about getting married and talk about our future. I didn't know what to think. So many times over the years, I wanted to kick him out. I daydreamed about living peacefully alone again. I was never lonely or unhappy when I lived on my own. However, I stayed the course because I loved Jose, even though I detested his behavior. I thought about Jose's daughter. She needed her father and me together, and I just couldn't abandon her. After she turned 18 and graduated high school, thoughts of letting go of the relationship returned. Things kept getting worse. My will was strong, my emotions stoic, but my body was feeling the anguish of it all, and it was taking a toll on my health.

As much as I really wanted to, I didn't dump him, because I was scared for HIM. If I kicked him out, would he go over the deep end with the drinking and kill himself? I never labeled Jose as an alcoholic. I knew to the very core of my being there was something driving his need to drink that he couldn't get control of. I felt it was something from his tumultuous and violent childhood. Something so disturbing that he couldn't cope with. He was so unhappy and anguished. It was heart-wrenching to watch and not be able to help in some way. I was at the end of my rope living like this, so when Jose came across the podcast where the guest found sobriety through an alternative treatment center in Mexico, I watched it right way. I <u>knew</u> it was the answer!

THE GIFT

PART FIVE
THE GIFT

Tragically, I became my father. An alcoholic full of resentment. It made sense. I come from a long line of alcoholics. My father, my grandfather, and other ancestors before them. At this point, I accepted my reality. I would live the rest of my life with sorrow and *rage*. I remember telling Samantha one evening that I felt I had a monster inside me. This great void of emptiness. I tried filling it with all kinds of toxic experiences. But alcohol was my preferred comfort. I felt powerless. Possessed by it.

I made so many promises, and I broke them all. Nobody trusted me anymore. My lies were catching up with me. I spent my time hiding my drinking and cleaning up my mess. I suffered from all the symptoms of PTSD. Fear consumed me. I constantly checked the same locks at night to make sure they were secure. At least ten times a night. Each lock over and over again.

The anxiety was the worst.

My dear Samantha was miserable under so much stress. Our relationship was dying. I was lying to her every day now. I felt as if I wore duct tape over my mouth when I was in the same room with her. My soul screamed for her. For help. For forgiveness. For her love.

There was only silence.

I would try to act sober. I was fooling no one. Especially her. She could smell it all over me. The way I was breathing. Talking too loudly. Cursing. Slurs. Lots of slurs. Swollen body. Broken mind.

Let me walk you through how bad I got.

I would go to lunch at a local bar. Eat my halibut tacos, chips, salsa, two double IPAs, and three shots of whiskey. Send out a few memes, answer a few emails, and hang out with my demons. *Feeling good*.

Then I would head over to the local brewery. Drink three bourbon barreled aged beers at 13% ABV. Those were the best.

Finally, heading home. *Feeling like a rock star.*

But first, a quick stop at the local liquor store to pick up some wine, beer, and spirits. The wine was to replace what I secretly stolen from our wine bar. Samantha knew what I was up to; I kept buying the wrong brand. The beer went in the fridge for later, and the spirits went inside my bathroom minibar.

At first, it was only one day a week. Then two, then three. Then pretty much Monday through Friday. Every time Samantha got home from work, she would find me a complete fuckin' mess. *She was heartbroken.*

The silence was the worst. How do you drown silence? With more spirits, *bathroom spirits.*

Our relationship seemed hopeless. I was losing the love of my life to my addiction.

In 2012, I experienced my first brush with death.

One evening in Ecuador, I went for a stroll in the middle of the night exposed to all the dark elements. While I was paying for a pack of smokes, the barrel of a gun was pressed into my ribs. I thought I was going to die that night. Then nothing. He patted me on the shoulder, grabbed the $20 from my hand and left. Just as silent as his arrival, he moved quietly into the darkness.

"Did you know that Kevlar laced string, aka professional kite string, can cut through plastic zip ties and possibly bone? You can literally saw off a head with a three-foot cord, if you put some elbow grease into it."

My second brush with death was in Mexico City in 2016. After a night of "entertaining" clients, I went for another evening stroll, searching for drugs. I was approached by a vehicle with two men and a woman inside. They asked if I wanted to buy some coke. I said, "HELL YEAH!" They said, "Cool." Their apartment was around the corner, and they invited me to go party with them. They had plenty of coke. Just before I got in the car, I felt this strange vibe and stopped. I started to walk backwards, and they got out of the car, trying to grab me. I was drunk but still able to evade and go back to my room. That night, I almost became a victim of human trafficking, organ donation, or worse.

"Did you know that in May 2020, a 72-year-old man by the name of Andres Mendoza was arrested in Atizapán de Zaragoza, north of Mexico City. During a raid to his home, the authorities discovered dismembered bodies, flayed skin, skulls, knives, and 20 recordings of murders he had committed. He was a serial killer and alleged cannibal. All women."

My office was located in Atizapán de Zaragoza, Mexico.

My third brush with death was again in Mexico City, May 2017. After another night "entertaining" clients and lots of whiskey, I went back to my hotel room. Food poisoning kept me up all night. The next morning, I called the lobby and asked if they stocked any Pepto Bismol. There was none to be had. So, I walked to the closest OXXO for my much-needed medication. I wobbled back to the hotel and went back to my room. *Something was horribly wrong!* I grabbed my wallet, keys, and phone and crawled down to the lobby to get an ambulance. Right before they made the call, I did a quick *hospitals near me* search on my cellphone. Out of all the choices, I selected Hospital Elizur. Since my phone was already in my hand, I automatically opened the UBER app and ordered a ride to the hospital. When I got there, the staff put me on a gurney, all the while running all kinds of tests. Within minutes, I was admitted.

"Did you know that if you do chest compressions after you stab someone in the heart, they die faster?"

My appendix was ready to burst. It was removed laparoscopically the next day, and I was back home a week later. As it turned out, Hospital Elizur specializes in gastrointestinal, abdominal, and laparoscopic appendix surgery. What were the odds?

I am alive today because of the amazing care by those doctors and the subtle still small voice that made me do a quick Google search. Had I not done so, my appendix would have ruptured inside the ambulance as it drove away into the unknown.

"Did you know that if you inject someone with opioids, they don't feel a thing? Especially the serrated edged blade as it cuts into their neck. They bleed out into pure bliss."

By the fall of 2019, I felt I was losing my mind. At first, I was suicidal. But that was not the route I chose to follow.

I became intrigued with death. I read about serial killers. I studied human trafficking, criminal tradecraft, and their methodologies. I was fascinated by all this knowledge. I could not get enough. Instagram was a great tool before they started censoring because it gave me access to some interesting people.

I began to distance myself from everyone. Full of rage and knowing what I was becoming. *Darkness!* Through the California Megan's Law Website, I accessed all local registered sex offenders in my area and surrounding cities. I was about to put them **ALL** on notice!

One morning, I sent highly disturbing messages to some friends. A few hours later, there was a knock on my door. My friend Lo came over. Only a hand full of people understand how my mind works, and he's one of them. He asked if there were any guns in the house. No. "Get dressed," he ordered. I assured him, "I'm okay." But he is a stubborn bastard. Just like me. He took me to lunch and sat with me until my madness settled down. I was in pretty bad shape.

Deep in the recesses of my soul, I knew I was not an alcoholic, and I was not the darkness that surrounded me. I was just broken, using alcohol as a coping mechanism for my trauma. I needed to find a solution.

That day, I made the decision to change my life.

I was determined to find a cure. I tried AA, psychotherapy, psychology, addiction therapy, group counseling, multiple churches, baptism, Brazilian Jiu-Jitsu, Cross Fit, volunteering, books, podcasts, white knuckling, and seclusion. Nothing worked. Finally, I tried prayer. *God, please help me find my way!*

On the morning of October 12, 2020, I was answering some emails at my desk and listening to episode 149 on the *Cleared Hot* podcast by Andy Stumpf. His guests were Andy Arrabito and Dan Cerrillo, both retired Navy SEALs. As I played it in the background as I usually do, I heard Mr. Cerrillo talk about his struggles with alcoholism and how he went to a treatment center in Mexico that was using Ibogaine to treat addiction. His story resonated in my bones. I immediately stopped what I was doing and turned the volume up. I sat there with a big smile on my face. *THIS IS IT!*

I had no idea what Ibogaine was, but I said, "Fuck it! I'm doing this."

In addition to being a bad ass SEAL and entrepreneur, Mr. Cerrillo is also the Chief of Staff for the American Addiction Center. I picked up the phone, called their hotline and left my contact information. Ibogaine is a Schedule 1 drug and illegal in the United States. They were going to refer me to the team in Cabo San Lucas, Mexico.

A week later, I get a call from Diane Baklor, co-Founder of The POI Institute.

"Hi, my name is Diane. How can I help?"

OMEGA

PART SIX
OMEGA

$7,500 dollars? Are you fucking serious?

This is a lot of money for me. I was broke. I told myself, *Forget it. Maybe next time!*

Negative. I need to do this. Think!

Later in the week, I received an email from my 401K provider. I was less than two weeks from paying off a 401K loan I took out last year to pay off my bar tabs. They offered me another opportunity to take out a new loan for $8,000 Dollars, at 2% interest. The timing of it all could not be any more perfect.

Boom! Money in the bank.

I called Diane Baklor and told her I was **ALL IN**.

On November 16, 2020, I jumped on a flight to Cabo San Lucas, Mexico, for alcohol abuse treatment at The POI Institute.

I was met at the airport by Diane and George. What a lovely couple! They drove me to a beautiful home overlooking the ocean next to a golf course. I then met Ma-Jo (short for Maria Jose). She too was a lovely human. They made me feel at home immediately.

First order of business. Bloodwork.

To my surprise, my tests came back all clear. My liver was in excellent condition.

I met the other house guests and enjoyed my first dinner in years where I was comfortable around complete strangers and still sober. I felt a sense of peace around me. This was on a Monday. The next morning at 9:00 am, I was in bed with an IV in my arm to keep me hydrated. I was also hooked up to an EKG machine to manage any possible cardiac abnormalities. They provided me with black-out eye shades and headphones with loud meditation music. My first dose of IBOGAINE was administered at 10:00 am. *And here we go...*

I was instantly transported to a realm where I was engulfed in gray clouds. Like giant gray anacondas circling around me. I found myself seated in an empty movie theater. Red velvet curtains. Popcorn, Reese's Pieces, and a Dr. Pepper in hand, I was about to watch a movie. The movie starts, and I see myself on the screen. Then, above and below the screen, tens of smaller TV's were also displaying my image on them. Different ages, different events. All simultaneously. *Whoa!*

My entire life was flashing before my eyes! I saw and felt it all.

At first, happy events were on the screen. Music, laughter, and good times. Next, some not so good events. Divorce, weekend dad, job losses. Then the events changed to a younger me. The main monitor showed my dad screaming at me. Hitting me.

Some life events did not display. The screen would remain blacked out. But I could feel the emotion behind them as if it were keeping me away from the pain.

I needed to pee. I will hold it. Fuck, never mind.

I took the shades off and looked at Ma-Jo. *Why is my body shaking? WTF?*

One of the common side effects of the drug is involuntary shakes. I could not walk properly, so I hugged the wall and wiggled my way to the bathroom. Another side effect is extreme thirst. But the IV was working too well. I must have peed at least ten times that night. I was so embarrassed. Poor Ma-Jo.

I put the shades and earphones back on. Ten year old Jose is now on display. Running around in the same pair of pants. Getting made fun of at school. I put the popcorn down and started to cry. I look to my right, and in my daze, Samantha is right there, holding my hand. I felt safe.

I looked further on and saw my grandfather and mother ... just a glimpse of them as they turned their backs towards me and walked away into the abyss.

Instantly, everything disappeared!

Darkness.

A golden skeleton key pops up.

I focused my attention on the key. Then my brain pops up... *Yeah, my brain, in gray.*

The key takes off flying, and I fly after it.

The key lands on a specific spot on the back of my brain. The Bermuda Triangle for memories. The brain dissolves away and a safe materializes with a golden padlock. The key unlocks the padlock, and the doors are blown open. I look inside the thick walls covered in rust and spider webs only to find two Polaroid pictures. I reached in and grabbed the first one. It was a photograph of me passed out face down in my underwear. *Some random room somewhere, I guess.* The second picture was difficult to make out. At first, all I saw was red. But after shifting my focus, I was able to make out an outline of a person screaming into a bathroom mirror. With sheer horror on their face. Crying. Then, I saw my tattoos. It was me. I was screaming into the mirror, frightened! Blood was everywhere!

A voice in the background was softly saying, *Pay Attention!*

I am back inside the movie theater. As I sat there, the screen displayed a flash back of me having a Skype video call with my good friend, Alejandro. The conversation went as follows.

"Dude, you drank a lot the other night. Are you OK? Do you remember what happened? You passed out in the lobby. Security had to take you up to the room in a wheelchair."

"Yeah, man. I don't remember much to be honest with you. What happened? I noticed you caught the early flight out. I saw the note. Is your wife OK?"

"Yes. Thanks for asking. She is fine. The accident was not as bad as she made it out to be. Sorry, I left without saying good bye. Anyhow, I just wanted to check in on you and make sure you were ok. Do you remember **anything** at all from that night?"

"Remember what? Dude, what happened?"

"Nothing. Hey listen, I have to run. I will call you next week to discuss a business lead I am sending you. If you could close it, it will generate a lot of revenue for your business."

"Hmm. OK, Bro. Thanks. Email me the information and I'll review it."

Right before we hung up, I swore I saw an evil grin on his face behind a shadow of darkness. I felt like throwing up. *Fuck, I hate hangovers.*

The voice was back.

This is it. Are you ready?

It then hit me like a freight train. Everything made sense. I sat in the movie theater alone this time. Screaming. Crying. Full of rage.

On the evening of January 7, 2010, after a long night of drinking in Las Vegas, I was **RAPED** by my "dear" friend and business mentor, Alejandro.

That night, I blacked out due to excessive drinking and ended up back in my hotel room. Which is strange because I never black out.

The howling woke me up. The bed was shaking, and I was paralyzed. Alejandro was a big guy. 6' 2" tall and 250 lbs., and he was on top of me. Sweating. Screaming. Possessed. *There was blood everywhere.*

I don't remember much after that point. It was all a blur. After he left, I managed to get to the bathroom, and the shock took over. I lost my mind that night.

Everything made sense now!

That's right, my child. The voice was back.

Yes. That happened to you. But it's OK. You are stronger than you think. You are not an alcoholic. You are not broken. You need to let this go now because we have important things to do.

I am not an alcoholic? I am not broken?

Correct.

You are love. You are light. You are infinite. Now let go…

When I opened my eyes, I saw Diane smiling at me. The first thing out of my mouth was, *I WAS RAPED! Tell Samantha I am going to be OK.*

I spent the next day and a half in bed, resting. Ibogaine beat the shit out of me. Mentally, emotionally, physically. It was now Thursday, and in three days, I lost ten pounds.

My 5-MeO-DMT* Ceremony was that evening. (*5 Methoxy N, N-dimethyltryptamine is a potent hallucinogen psychoactive ten times the relative potency found in the DMT vines used to make Ayahuasca.

This particular 5-MeO-DMT is found in the venom of the Bufo Alvarius toad of the Sonoran Desert)

A magical frog, Águila *the Shaman,* Uggs the Cat, and the Death of my Ego.

Águila tells me to count backward from ten.

I made it to five.

My mind imploded. I was in outer space traveling the cosmos. I went to the end of time to an event where six celestial beings were using their powers to control supernovas from exploding. Each had their own Death Star. *WTF?* As I floated in space viewing this epic scene, the first being died. BOOM! The first Supernova goes off. Followed by the next, and the next. A domino effect. I knew that if it hit the last remaining one, it would be the end. The end of **everything! THE VOLTRONIC DESTRUCTION OF THE UNIVERSE!**

I jumped on the last Death Star and used my body to absorb the impact. Time to die. As I was ready to be turned into star dust, I was grabbed by all the celestial beings. They told me to let go. It would be OK. To trust them. *I let myself go ...*

Did I mention that I was walking around like a zombie around this time? Yup. Somewhere after passing out and lying on a blanket, I stood up, walked around, moved furniture around, went up to people, and stared at them. It was shortly after that I stood tall and screamed at the top of my lungs; **We are all FUCKED**! I then passed out.

All I remember was the warm, blinding light engulfing me.

Then there was silence.

I woke up with the biggest smile on my face and a sense of peace. As if reborn. Hard to describe it. As I looked around the room, everyone was staring at me stunned. In addition to sleep walking, I managed to put the Shaman's wife in half guard (a jiu-jitsu ground position). She was okay! I wrapped around her legs and hips, and they could not get me off her. Luckily, nobody was harmed. I find it pretty funny, if you ask me.

After we talked about what I experienced, we determined that the supernovas were my ego being destroyed. It makes sense. If it's not over the top, I don't want any part of it. ☺

On a macro level, Ibogaine allowed me to unlock the secrets to my pain. The event that changed my life and nearly took everything I held dear, including my life. It allowed me to process the experience and let it go. To move on. It also repaired my brain from all the harm I caused it. The 5-MeO-DMT repaired my soul. It reset my mind and gave me the freedom to live life without fear and doubt. These two holy medicines performed a beautiful cosmic surgery on me. They brought me back to life.

To Diane, George, Ma-Jo, Águila, his wife, and Uggs the Cat, I am forever grateful for you being the team to bring me back to life. I love you!

To the other house members I was honored to meet, may you continue to be the light. I hope our paths cross again in this life or the next.

After our hugs goodbye, Diane told me I needed to continue to exercise but most importantly, talk to someone that would help me cope with the knowing of what happened to me.

Technically, my sobriety date is November 8, 2020. That was the last day I drank an alcoholic beverage. But I celebrate the 19th. The night I did 5-MeO-DMT. The day of my awakening. I was not the same person anymore...

Every negative thought, depression, anxiety, guilt, fear, rage, resentment, every lie, every addiction was gone.

Arriving in Los Angeles a few days later, without a care in the world, I was a gentle flow moving through the chaos of Hollywood Burbank Airport.

When I got home, I was *finally* able to *see* Samantha. I kissed her, and embraced her in a loving hug. We sat down on the couch and everything poured out of me. I told her about Diane, George, and Ma-Jo, Uggs the cat. Aguila the Shaman, and his wife. My Ibogaine and 5-MeO-DMT experience. Finally, I told her what Alejandro did to me in Las Vegas. It came out so carefree. Her mouth dropped for a second, followed by silence, then finally she said, "It all makes sense."

"This is when your drinking got bad. I have known you for a long time and have been around your drinking. You were fun. A goofball. Safe. After you were raped, you became angry, deceitful, and an asshole. I knew you were not an alcoholic, and you tried so hard to find a solution. When you had me listen to the podcast, I knew this was it."

That was ten months ago. What an amazing journey it has been.

I gave up drinking.

Alcohol makes me crazy and awakens the monster still inside me.

I consumed enough alcohol to last several lifetimes. I was done!

If you are hurting and are using alcohol to cope, talk to someone, please. Ask for help. Your future self will thank you for it. I know it's scary. But know this, you have the entire universe in your soul. Standing up for yourself is the most courageous thing a person can do. Have faith and invest in you.

I went to counseling.

Rev. Dr. Maureen Hoyt (my co-author) helped me make sense of it all. To communicate. Three months into our sessions, she fired me. Told me to not to come back. That I was good …

I got fit and healthy.

I made a commitment to get in shape. The team at Persistent Culture in Moorpark, CA, were the perfect team. Gaige, the Head Coach, developed a specific program to achieve and surpass my goals. Ciara, my Nutritionist got my macros down perfectly. My buddy Christian, inspired me to get abs. I dropped 47 lbs. with their help. You might want to check them out. They do cool things.

I got better at Jiu-Jitsu.

What can I say about Professor Arnaldo Maidana, Owner and Head Instructor of Checkmat Northridge, CA? He is a rock star. Over six feet tall and floating around 215 lbs., he moves like a ninja. His flow is impressive. His Jiu Jitsu is out of this world. My bro Dory "The Lebanese Tiger" Aoun kept telling me to join this academy. I kept brushing it off. Finally, on June 4, 2020, I attended my first class as a new student. I was 190.3 lbs. that day. After getting murdered by everyone, I asked him to take my blue belt and give me a white one. These men and women were savages. Sixteen months later, I am on a flight heading to Dallas to compete at the IBJJF World NO GI Championships. My game has improved by leaps and bounds because of him. Come check out a class if you're in the Reseda/Northridge area. You might just love it.

Finances

Remember that debt I accumulated on Samantha's credit? Nearly gone. My job is doing well. Numbers are up and costs are down. My

3rd business is doing great. Running efficiently and profitable. Samantha gives me a hard time because I only work two hours a day. What can I say, I like to optimize things. There is abundance in our lives now. Our income is now secondary. It took me 44 years to finally understand how money works and how to respect it. Our primary goal is now to live our lives full of joy and help others achieve their potential.

Relationships

I have surrounded myself with amazing humans. Each with unique talents and gifts to share with this world. I am inspired by them every day. My circle is now even smaller. I have chosen quality versus quantity. I am a natural giver, a provider, a doer of good deeds. Always have been and always will. Sometimes, I give a bit too much and get taken advantage of, but that's okay. I see the lessons in it and try my hardest not to repeat it. I have learned to set boundaries, and I know when to say no.

Alejandro and my father

I needed to shed myself of all that pain and move forward. The only way possible was to forgive them both. I understand why they did what they did. They were mentally ill individuals full of pain and addiction. Remember back in Part Two, I said that *I wanted to be like Alejandro one day!* Well, guess what, in my addiction, I was becoming him. So, choose wisely when you talk to yourself. Regardless if it's a positive comment or a negative one. You will get what you ask for.

I wish them peace.

Rosa

I cannot fathom how difficult it must have been for you, having to take on the burden of raising two uninvited kids. Yet, you powered through and provided my sister and me with a roof over our heads, food on the table, and a family. You sacrificed a lot for us. I have grit because of you. I'm sorry I never have told you but, you have always been my mother. *La amo...*

My Siblings

I miss you. Hope we can connect soon.

My Samantha

"I look at her and light goes all through me."
– **Charles Bukowski**

Our relationship is healed. We are having a blast together! I love her so much, and I tell her every day. I don't travel as much for work anymore, only when it's important. I need her close.

We talk now. We collaborate. We travel. We swim with dolphins, hang out with Shamans, take 5-MeO DMT together, talk about the future, goals, how to influence others in a larger scale. We pray together. We meditate together. We hold ceremony together. Her body is healing and looks years younger. She has lost 15 lbs. by eating clean, exercising, and living a stress-free life. (Mostly my stress). She trusts me now. She is my Alpha and Omega.

Activities

These are some of the cool things I am now into:

Drumming, skating, coaching, energy healing, photoshopping friends into funny memes, shamanism, reading, mentoring, and now writing. *I do have a favorite. Can you guess what that is?*

It's as if my brain can process data more efficiently. Meaning, I don't see things as difficult anymore. I see them as just levels of knowing. The more I do something I love, the more quickly I pick it up... With every decision I now make, I ask myself:

Is this fun? Will it make me be a better person? Can I optimize it?

I am a completely different Jose. I still have a strong ego and the crazy monster inside me. But Samantha helps to keep them both in check. Now, my soul is on fire!

We all coexist in harmony...

Each of us has a specific role to play. My healthy ego drives innovation. I keep us wholesome and mindful. My Spirit inspires others through love.

This book was extremely emotional to write, yet so much fun. It gave me closure.

Yes, in some ways, my life has had tragic moments, but I also have enjoyed some amazing experiences. I became a Marine. I hold records.

I started several businesses and ran only one of them into the ground. I have been addicted to a laundry list of things. I met some of the most amazing people all over the world. I was both "The Class Clown" and "Most Athletic." Almost shit my pants in front of an audience over a prank. Survived multiple kidnap attempts. Held up at gun point. Worked next to a serial killer. Been broke as fuck. Now live in abundance. I've been obese. I now have abs. For a brief moment in time, I lost my rational mind and contemplated killing people.

Now, I just flow.

If I had to go through all that pain over again to get just **one** opportunity to be the person I am now, would I?

Abso-fucking-lutely!

Knowing this, I would like to offer some cool advice. Let me get my ego to join us in this exercise. That dude is funny...

I'll go first.

Be kind to each other

Ego: Don't be an asshole

See the lessons in every struggle

Ego: Take risks

Be a warrior in the garden

Ego: Act accordingly

Be true to your word

Ego: Bring Blockbuster back

Intent + Action = Manifestation (Read that again!)

Ego: I have abs (*Read that again!*)

Be the change

Ego: Prius drivers can only drive in the slow lane.

AND ABOVE ALL ELSE...

Love yourself first!

Ego: Don't be an asshole...

Thank you so much for taking this journey with me. I pray my story gives you hope. If this beautiful, XL, psychotic, alcoholic can change, so can you!

So live your life that the fear of death can never enter your heart.

Trouble no one about their religion; respect others in their view, and demand that they respect yours.

Love your life, perfect your life, beautify all things in your life.

Seek to make your life long and its purpose in the service of your people. Prepare a noble death song for the day when you go over the great divide.

Always give a word or a sign of salute when meeting or passing a friend, even a stranger, when in a lonely place.

Show respect to all people and bow to none.

When you arise in the morning, give thanks for the food and for the joy of living. If you see no reason for giving thanks, the fault lies only in yourself.

Abuse no one and nothing, for abuse turns the wise ones to fools and robs the spirit of its vision. When it comes your time to die, be not like those whose hearts are filled with fear of death, so that when their time comes they weep and pray for a little more time to live their lives over again in a different way.

Sing your death song and die like a hero going home."

Chief Tecumseh, 1768 – 1813

ACKNOWLEDGEMENTS

I used to live my life in fear. Full of anxiety, depression, and hate. Constantly making wrong choices and blaming everyone but myself.

It truly takes a village. But it starts with a choice. A choice to be a better version of yourself. I celebrate my old self every day. I honor him in everything that I do now. For he had the most courage. The courage to change his life for the better.

I am grateful to Lo, for showing up. This story would be completely different if you had not. Andy Stumpf for episode 149 on your Cleared Hot podcast. Mr. Dan Cerrillo for sharing your story. It resonated in my bones. Maynard James Keenan, for your wonderful lyrics. The POI Institute for giving me peace. Dory Aoun and Elder Cruz for your fearlessness. I am so proud of you both. Professor Arnaldo Maidana for your patience and guidance. Rev. Dr. Maureen Hoyt for our conversations and your help in co-writing this book with me. The entire team at Persistence Culture, for getting me in shape. My teammates at Checkmat, it is an honor to step on the mats with you. My daughter Celeste for being my cheerleader, and my Samantha. For not giving up on me.

Lastly, dear reader. Thank you for investing your time and resources to read this story. I appreciate you 🩶

Love and Light...

Jose

This is not the END. It's clearly the beginning.

Let's GO!

ABOUT THE AUTHORS

Jose Torres currently lives in Moorpark, California with his wife Samantha Cosney and their three fur babies Maddie, Jaxx, and Uggs. If he is not practicing on the drums you will find him training Brazilian Jiu-Jitsu at Checkmat Northridge.

You can follow him on Instagram or Facebook @josetoresbjj or his website: www.acosmicsurgery.com

Rev. Dr. Maureen Hoyt is an ordained minister of Religious Science and has been awarded both a Doctor of Religious Science and a Doctor of Divinity for exceptional service with the Centers for Spiritual Living. She has been in active ministry for 24 years and a practitioner for 30 years in that movement. Over the years, she has received every possible award from the organization for service above and beyond the call of duty. She was formerly president of International New Thought Alliance, Los Angeles, and has been active with Institute of Noetic Sciences, founded by astronaut Edgar Mitchell, on and off for over 25 years. In March 2017, she presented on the IONS cruise to Mexico and was well-received. She recently taught a portion of the Ministerial Studies Program for the Holmes Institute. She continues to speak as a substitute at local centers every month and is teaching various metaphysical classes as the demand arises. Her practice as a counselor/coach is a significant part of her desire to make a difference in the world, and this aspect of her life continues to be incredibly rewarding.

For approximately eight years, she was the Editorial Coordinator for the in-house magazine, *Creative Thought*, which was published monthly. After retirement from pulpit ministry, she reinvented herself as an in-demand editor/proofreader and is enjoying going back to her roots. She lives in Westlake Village, CA, close to her children, Heather and Nathan, and her adored granddaughter, Sydney

You can follow her on Facebook @maureen.hoyt.9 or on her website at www.drmaureenhoyt.com

For more information on The POI Institute Ibogaine Treatment Center Mexico, visit their website at: www.poiibogaine.com

A COSMIC PLAN
A WORKBOOK BY JOSE TORRES

In the last year, my life has completely changed, including my physical appearance and my mindset. I have dropped 60 lbs., competed in THREE Brazilian Jiu-Jitsu World Championships, *Medaled in TWO*, wrote a book, and launched several wellness items under my product line Cosmic Mist™. I surrounded myself with incredible people of unique talents. Yes, my treatment at The POI Institute in Cabo, Mexico, provided me a new opportunity to live life the way I always dreamed. Fearless and with my past behind me. But it was the effort I achieved after that allowed me to live a life full of creativity, joy, and abundance.

Let's look at what I did.

I started by SETTING AN INTENTION!

NOW THAT I AM SOBER, WHO CAN I BECOME?

I wrote down my goals. I am going to do the following:

1. GET IN SHAPE.
2. COMPETE IN A WORLD CHAMPIONSHIP IN JIU-JITSU
3. WRITE A BOOK
4. STUDY SPIRITUALITY
5. DO COOL SHIT

Now that I had my goals written down, I aligned myself with the right people to help me achieve those goals, and I WENT TO WORK.

- I HIRED A NUTRITIONIST.
- I TRAINED JIU-JITSU SIX DAYS A WEEK AND BOOKED PRIVATE SESSIONS WITH WORLD CHAMPIONS.
- I LIFTED WEIGHTS THREE DAYS A WEEK, TWO HOURS EACH DAY.
- I MEDITATED.
- I SAID A GRATITUDE PRAYER EVERY NIGHT BEFORE BED.

- I READ INSPIRING BOOKS.
- I STOPPED HANGING OUT WITH ASSHOLES.
- I STOPPED DWELLING ON THE PAST.
- I STARTED **HAVING FUN.**

When I started taking care of myself, I began to feel better, I looked better, and I attracted better people and experiences. It all started within me. Therefore, because of my sobriety, I developed clarity of mind, and I focused on improving THREE specific areas in my life.

1. MINDFULNESS
2. MENTAL HEALTH
3. PHYSICAL HEALTH

By focusing on these THREE areas consistently, I became the man I always wanted to be. I stopped living in fear and started LIVING in joy! A year ago, if you told me that I would have abs at 45 years old, my response would have been, "You must be on crack!" Yet, here I stand, pushing 45, and in the best shape of my life. People I have known for many years don't recognize me! That's how impactful my transformation has been.

My publisher challenged me to come up with a workbook to go along with my story. They wanted some form of guide any reader can follow to successfully transform their life. After giving it some thought, I asked myself, *what would I say if I had the world's attention for 15 Minutes?*

I give you, **A Cosmic Plan**.

What is a Cosmic Plan?

A Cosmic Plan is a guide for those individuals looking for sustainable change, a plan so simple anyone can follow and apply it. With consistency, the right attitude, and effort, you too can transform your life.

All you have to do is: **PUT IN THE WORK!**

Let's dive into the specific things I did during my year of transformation, starting with:

MINDFULNESS

Something awakened inside me during my psychedelic treatment. I connected with my own consciousness. Some call it GOD, Brahman, Jesus, Infinite Intelligence, Spirit, Allah, and many more. I call it the **I AM**.

Since we are all cosmic beings having a human experience, I wanted to understand what I tapped into. Was it unique to me or could others experience this awakening?

I had several questions:

What is my life's purpose?

How can a plant and frog venom cure my alcoholism, where other methods could not?

Why am I so easily able to let go of all the pain Alejandro and my father caused me?

So, I bought and read books. A lot of books. I started with Spirituality, then Shamanism, followed by Psychedelic Medicine. Each night, I performed a Gratitude Ceremony where I prayed, meditated, and gave thanks for all the experiences and blessings in my day and my life. I burned tobacco, sage, palo santo, and used basil for smudging our room to cleanse prior negative energies during and after each ceremony.

Are you familiar with Binaural Beats? They are healing, transformational, and connecting frequencies. Every night for the past year, I played them in the background as Samantha and I slept. I found this channel to have very good options on YouTube. **Good Vibes – Binaural Beats**. They have one, in particular, I use daily. It is twelve hours long, enough to last all night. Search YouTube for "**6 Tones of Creation Good Vibes.**" There are several meditation backdrops to choose from under this title.

By listening to these tones while I sleep, I have become more in-tune with myself. I feel more creative, understand things quickly, and attract the most amazing people into my circle of influence.

Below are the Binaural Beat Frequencies and my understanding of their purpose:

396 Hz –Turning Grief into Joy. Liberating Guilt and Fear

417 Hz – Undoing Situations and Facilitating Changes

528 Hz – Transformation and Miracles and DNA Repair

639 Hz – Re-Connecting and Balancing Relationships

741 Hz – Problem Solving, Expressions, and Solutions

852 Hz – Awakening Intuition, Love, and Spiritual Order.

In addition to the above, I recommend the following **Action Items** be done on a daily basis:

MEDITATE

Be in silence for 10-15 min a day. Any time of day that works for you.

Sit in a comfortable and quiet environment.

Observe any colors, shapes, thoughts, sounds, and feelings you may experience.

Don't feel bad if NOTHING happens. ***Observing*** that nothing happens is also good.

Just **observe**.

Note: I like to use blacked-out eyeshades and noise-canceling head-phones. At times, I also play meditation music in the background. If you also prefer music, I recommend "Mapping the Cosmos" by DEYA DOVA. It's just over eight minutes. Enough time to get a quick meditation and escape into her world. I put it on auto-repeat for meditation lasting longer than eight minutes and put the timer on my phone to whatever length I am going to meditate.

Please feel free to seek your own meditation method. There are endless choices available for little or no cost. Follow your heart and you will find what is best for you.

 Quick Tip

Creating a Playlist with your favorite meditation music allows you to access it easily at home or on the go via your cellphone or other digital devices. You can always add/delete songs as you evolve in your meditation journey.

BE IN GRATITUDE

As I mentioned earlier, I perform a Gratitude Ceremony each night since I came back from Cabo, Mexico. My goal was to verbally express my thanks for my experiences throughout the day and appreciate the blessings in my life, including the challenges. Once again, the difficulties of life hold valuable lessons to be learned. Here are some more **Action Items I recommend** you do on a daily basis.

Before going to bed, do a gratitude prayer.

Give thanks for the day.

Give thanks for your friends and loved ones.

Give thanks for the challenges in your life.

CONNECT WITH YOUR HIGHER POWER

When I started thinking in terms of inclusiveness, love, generosity, and being of service, I started to feel better about myself. I started to attract better things into my life. My life in general got better.

Read. Go to Church. Pray.

 Quick Tip

Next time you are at Walmart or any bargain store, buy a couple of XL Hoodies and keep them in your car. The next time you see a homeless person who may need one, gift them a Hoodie. They will appreciate it, and you will feel good.

MENTAL HEALTH

Mental health for me meant changing the way I looked at external factors that caused me stress, anxiety, and depression. I surrounded myself with individuals who were negative, lacked ambition, and were addicted to alcohol. I used alcohol to create a false sense of reality, being popular, successful, and surrounded by people who supported my alcoholism. The truth was that I burned a lot of bridges, I was financially broke, and most of the people I associated with were toxic individuals.

SEEK HELP

Seek the help that is most comfortable for you and do it. That could be joining a church, talking to a professional therapist, Psychedelics, and/or AA. **DO SOMETHING!**

LET GO OF TOXIC RELATIONSHIPS

Stop hanging out with the following individuals who:

- Complain about everything
- Always gossip

- Always have an opinion about your life
- Are always angry
- Lack ambition and drive

CHANGE YOUR THINKING

All the negative self-talk, judgments toward others, and assumptions about life were the most challenging behaviors for me to transition out of. I conditioned myself to believe in divisiveness and a selfish "every person for himself" mentality.

Stop criticizing yourself. Every thought CREATES and WORDS can cast spells. That is why they refer to it as SPELLING. The more you THINK and TALK negatively about yourself, the more you will experience the negativity in life. YOU will create a state of DEPRESSION, LACK, and NEED. So, THINK and TALK **POSITIVELY** about yourself.

Why not, you are perfect and deserve it!

Stop judging others. Focus your energy on beautifying all things in your life. Don't waste time making judgments. They serve no one.

Stop making assumptions. Focus on the present moment and deal with issues as they happen. Stop creating false narratives and expectations in your head. You are just creating FAKE NEWS.

Quick Tip

Stop saying "**I WANT.**" Instead, say **I AM BECOMING, I HAVE**, or simply say **I AM.**

PHYSICAL HEALTH

When I made the decision to get healthier, I tried many things. I started training up to six days a week at my Jiu-Jitsu Academy, did three CrossFit workouts a week, and began fasting. But I was tired ALL the time. I remember one day I fell asleep in my truck in the parking lot after practice because I was so fatigued. My decision to hire a Professional Nutritionist changed everything about my vitality. She told me I was calorie deficit. Meaning I was not consuming enough calories to maintain my daily activities. After I explained my training goals to her, she went to work and outlined my MACROS (short for Macronutrients). They are the three categories of nutrients we eat the most and provide us with most of our energy: protein, carbohydrates, and fats. When we are counting macros, we're counting the grams of protein, carbs, and fats we're consuming. With my macros done, I hired a meal prep company to provide my lunch and dinners with those specific macros. I drink a protein shake for breakfast and post workouts. I started taking supplements like Amino Acids, Glutamine, and Creatine. The pounds came right off. My goal was to reduce from 190 lbs. to 175 lbs. I ended up weighing in at 143 lbs. at my lightest.

EAT HEALTHIER

You are what you eat! Period. So be mindful of what you put in your body. Stop eating junk food on a daily basis. Eat a protein-packed breakfast. Get a nutritionist to help you understand how to tailor a plan that will maximize your results.

GET ACTIVE

MOVE. SWEAT. LIFT WEIGHTS

This pandemic has shown that as a society, we have a health problem.

To combat disease and variants, lose weight, gain muscle, and live stress- free.

CONNECT WITH MOTHER EARTH

Go outdoors.

Breathe fresh air.

Get some sun.

Go for a walk.

Talk to plants.

Walk barefoot on grass or in the sand at the beach.

Quick Tip

If you are looking for a good protein shake, I recommend to all my friends the MRE Meal Replacement Protein Powder by REDCON1. It has 5g Fat, 75g Carbs, and 47g Protein. It's like drinking a meal.

A COSMIC PLAN

Sit in silence for a few minutes and ask, **_WHO DO I WANT TO BE IN ONE YEAR?_**

My Intention Is to be: _____

_____

_____

_____

What do YOU think you need to do to achieve that?

1. _____

_____

_____

_____

2. _____

_____

_____

_____

3. _____

_____

_____

_____

4. _____

_____

_____

_____

5. _____

_____

_____

_____

Prioritize those goals, action items, and do them. Find joy and appreciation for these tasks. The food may taste bland, you will pee more frequently (because you now drink more water), and you will not want to lift those weights. That's when you remind yourself that you have work to do.

Once you have the VISION (the whole view of your goals and what you need to do), you can then start to WORK towards your INTENTION and ACHIEVE IT.

NOW PUT IN THE WORK!

Love and Light,

Jose and Samantha

A COSMIC JOURNAL

This simple daily exercise will allow you to monitor your progress during your Cosmic Journey of self-transformation. Use this tool to reflect and help guide you to better choices. You can keep this format or develop your own as you see fit.

Name:

Week:

Day:

Date:

Sleep: ____ Hrs

Quality: 1-10 _____

Binaural Beats? Y/N

Which one:

_____

Did you have any dreams that you remember? Y/N

If so, write it down:

_____

Meditation.

Y/N

Length (Minutes) 5/10/15+

Did you feel/see/hear anything?

If so, write it down:

_____

_____

Did you use Music in the background: (Y/N)

Mental Health

Stress Level: 1 2 3 4 5 6 7 8 9 10

Anxiety Level: 1 2 3 4 5 6 7 8 9 10

Write down (3) things you like about yourself.

1. _____

2. _____

3. _____

Write down (3) things you need to improve on yourself.

1. _____

2. _____

3. _____

Write down your Affirmation of the Day:

_____

_____

_____

I AM IMPROVING ON THE FOLLOWING (3) THINGS WITH EASE, GRACE, AND WITH LOVE:

_____

_____

_____

Reading
Name of Book: _____

Minutes Read: _____

Physical Activity
Today I did:

_____

_____

_____

Hydration (Color of Urine) 10 being clear

1 2 3 4 5 6 7 8 9 10

Alcohol: Y/N

Junk Food: Y/N

Evening
Light a Candle, Play your Meditation Music in the background, and give Thanks for the:

- Day.
- Your Life.
- Your loved ones.
- Your Friends
- Your challenges (They give you wisdom)

NOTES: